Easy Phonics

A Cockroach in the Coach

and other stories

OA IE EE

AF621186

2d

by Tapasi De

Illustrated by Suman S. Roy

ABOUT PHONICS

Phonics is the understanding that there is an important relationship between the letters or graphemes of the written language and the individual sounds or phonemes of the spoken language.

A strong knowledge of phonics helps a child considerably to recognize these relationships, to recognize familiar words accurately and automatically, and also "decode" new words. This knowledge substantially improves the reading ability of the child.

In the *Easy Phonics* series, the basic 48 sounds of English have been dealt with through stories. The series is divided into 4 levels with 4 books in each level. Each book contains 2-3 stories based on a particular sound. Colourful illustrations and the repetition of a particular sound ringing through the story make this series absolutely unique!

CONTENTS

A COCKROACH IN THE COACH

OA as in GOAT

Sammy the cockroach is driving his coach. He is wearing a coat. He is going to fetch his friends for his birthday party.

The road is lined with oak trees. Sammy is having a toast in his coach. He is hungry.

Suddenly he sees his friend, a stoat, run by. He calls out to the stoat. A little later a goat and a foal also join Sammy.

They all have a lot of fun in the coach. Just then, Sammy hears a croak. He peeps out and sees a toad. The toad is his friend too.

The toad is floating on a large leaf in a pond. He is eating a roasted bug. He also joins the cockroach in the coach.

The cockroach gets a motorboat as his birthday gift! He treats his friends to oatcakes and juice. It is a wonderful day for the cockroach.

Words with the 'OA' sound

soak	cloak	goal	foal
foam	loan	soap	boast
coast	road	coal	groan
moat	gloat	groan	hoarse
loaf	poach	shoal	throat
coaster	boat	float	load

THE THIEF MAGPIE

IE as in FIELD/PIE

Julie the magpie is a thief. She steals food for her meals every day.

One day Willie, the chief of magpies, calls Julie. He asks her to steal grains from the farmer Charlie's granary.

Julie flies to Charlie's farm at night. Quietly, she enters the granary and steals grains.

With the help of her friend Marie, Julie steals a lot of grains. When the chief magpie Willie comes to know this, he is very happy.

The chief tells Julie that she should now try to steal the cookies baked by Charlie's wife.

Julie takes the help of her niece to steal the cookies. The stealing goes on for many days.

Meanwhile, Charlie and his wife are worried to find their grains and cookies missing every day.

Charlie and his wife believe that they should keep a pet dog. So they bring a dog, who spies on the granary day and night.

Now Julie is too confident that no one could catch her. But she does not know about the fierce pet of Charlie.

The pet dog Donnie is very smart. On his very first night at the granary, he catches Julie. She cries but in vain. Charlie is relieved.

Words with the 'IE' sound

pie	lie	tie	die
diesel	cries	pier	tier
flies	wield	field	yield
shield	tries	spies	thief
chief	niece	brief	grief
piece	relief	siege	priest
cookie	fiend	eerie	pierce

THE BEETLE AND THE QUEEN BEE

EE as in THREE

Edith is a honeybee and Evan is a beetle. They are best friends.

One day Evan the beetle visits the honeycomb where Edith lives. There he sees the queen bee Sheena in her pretty green gown.

Evan falls in love with her and wants to marry her. Queen Sheena smiles and welcomes him into her honeycomb.

That night Evan the beetle does not sleep. He keeps thinking about the sweet smile of Queen Sheena.

When the other animals of the jungle like the sheep, the deer and the cheetah hear about this, they all laugh.

The next day Evan decides to please the queen. He gifts her tree leaves, coffee beans and beetroot. When Sheena comes to know about Evan's deep feelings, she is amused.

Edith tells Evan that he cannot marry the queen as he is a beetle! But it is of no use. Evan goes on to buy three dresses for the queen.

As time passes by, even the queen falls in love with Evan. Then, one day, Evan meets Sweenie, a beautiful beetle. He begins to like her.

Queen Sheena feels sad when she hears this. Evan and Sweenie get married and live happily.

Words with the 'EE' sound

geese	heel	been	beer
creek	beef	beet	breed
bleed	deep	deer	cheer
creep	career	eerie	fleet
agree	deed	flee	free
cheek	feed	feet	feel
fleece	greed	glee	freeze

LET'S RECALL

1. Where is Sammy the cockroach going in his coach?

2. What is the toad eating?

3. What does the cockroach get as his birthday gift?

4. Who is the chief of magpies?

5. Where does Julie steal grains from?

6. How does Julie get caught?

7. What is queen bee Sheena wearing when Evan the beetle visits her?

8. What does Evan the beetle gift to queen Sheena?